MEDICINE IN CRISIS

A DOCTOR'S CONCERNS

GW00545679

Dr. Sheila L. M. Gibson, M.D., B.Sc., M.F.Hom.

**Illustrated
by
Liz Vaughan**

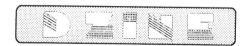

ISBN 0-9543771-1-7

Design & Print by

268 Bath Street, Glasgow. G2 4JR
Tel/Fax: 0141 332 8507

DEDICATION

This book is dedicated to my late husband Dr. Robin Gordon Gibson who introduced me to some of the techniques which I currently practise, and with whom I explored many others. Each of us has added our own particular angles and expertise to the body of knowledge contained within these pages, but without his help and influence this book could not have been written.

ACKNOWLEDGEMENT

I wish to express my grateful thanks to my friends and colleagues Dr. Ramona Sue, Mrs. Mary Black and Mrs. Liz Vaughan for their invaluable help in refining the typescript.

CONTENTS

MEDICINE IN CRISIS; A DOCTOR'S CONCERNS

INTRODUCTION

When the National Health Service was inaugurated in 1948, it was confidently predicted that the health of the nation would be vastly improved within just a few years. Health care became freely available to all, new drugs to treat illness were being developed, everything in the garden appeared rosy.

Unfortunately the promises remain unfulfilled. After over 50 years of the NHS, the health of the nation is poorer than it was in 1948. People may be living longer, though this is debateable, but they are certainly not living more healthily. Not only are people less healthy, but the NHS itself is struggling to keep alive. What has gone wrong?

A major problem is that modern medicine focuses on disease removal rather than health maintenance; and disease removal concentrates on giving chemicals (drugs) to combat disease thus treating the symptoms rather than the cause of the problem. These chemicals tend to suppress the symptoms and signs of the disease, giving a semblance of improvement but in reality driving the problems deeper into the body's metabolic infrastructure. Modern medicine has yet to learn that synthetic chemicals can never CURE disease. Not only that, but most, if not all, of them are associated with toxic side effects which in turn require other chemicals to counteract them. This is an expensive and counterproductive approach to health care and is a major reason for the current unhealthy state of the NHS.

Much of this problem stems from the orthodox view of health and disease and this we shall look at now.

THE ORTHODOX PARADIGM

The official establishment view of a human being is that we are an ingenious collection of chemicals cleverly put together to form the cells, tissues and organs of our bodies. Our inherited patterns are encoded in the DNA of our genes, which are also chemicals. These direct the synthesis of the building blocks of our cells, and all their subcellular components, which aggregate to form our tissues and organs. Our nerves work by electrical impulses which depend on other chemicals for their generation and our moods and feelings are dependent on yet another set of chemicals, our hormones. Our thoughts and perceptions depend on electrical impulses in the brain. Again these depend on more chemicals.

This mechanistic view reduces all living beings to an intricate system of inter-related and interacting chemicals. This being the case, it is not surprising that illness should be viewed as a wrong functioning, basically, of our chemical processes and that the logical approach to treatment should be other chemicals which can correct what has gone wrong. It therefore comes as a shock to many that this logical, chemical approach is not producing miraculous cures. Rather it is producing an increasing burden of ill-health.

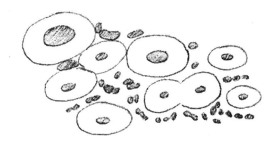

THE ALTERNATIVE/COMPLEMENTARY VIEW

Before the advent of the Age of Reason in the eighteenth century, few would have disputed the idea that human beings were more than just a physical body; that they had a soul and/or spirit, which supplied the life force, or vital force, which animates the body in life and withdraws at death.

With increasing scientific knowledge of how the body works, and what it is composed of, this idea became increasingly ridiculed since no-one could find the soul or spirit, and it was therefore assumed that such things did not exist. Man was just a clever collection of chemicals.

However, interest in communicating with the dead through mediums in trance, out of body experiences, near death experiences and possible evidence for reincarnation, beginning in the latter part of the nineteenth century, and continuing until the present day, has produced a substantial body of so-called paranormal experiences which are difficult to explain in purely mechanistic terms. It is likely that not all of this evidence is genuine, but there is a sufficient amount which does appear to be so, to raise questions about the true nature of living beings.

The development of Quantum Theory by Niels Bohr, Albert Einstein and others in the late nineteenth and early twentieth centuries confirmed that the physical world is not the solid, material structure that we suppose it to be. It seems that things are not necessarily what they appear to be. Any schoolchild should now know, that "solid" matter is not really solid but contains far more space than actual matter, and that matter itself is made up of electrical charges held together in ingenious ways by mysterious forces which are still not completely understood. Matter is not at all what it seems and much of it may be undetectable to us.

There are a number of somewhat differing views of the make up of a living being. The following is a scheme which is generally accepted in most alternative/complementary circles.

Our densest part, the one with the lowest vibrational level, is our familiar physical body composed of the various biological building blocks, cells, tissues and organs, obeying the laws of biochemistry, and organised and kept functioning by our nervous system, enzymes, hormones and other messenger chemicals on which cell to cell communication depends. But what keeps these components functioning harmoniously? Obviously it is our DNA. But what originated and controls the DNA?

At a higher vibratory level than the physical is the life body, or etheric body which is visualised as interpenetrating the physical body and projecting slightly beyond it. This is considered to be the level of the vital force or life force and it forms the innermost layer of the aura. At a higher vibratory level is the emotional body, then the mental body, and highest of all, vibrationally speaking, is the spiritual body or spiritual self. These subtle bodies are invisible to most of us but can be seen by some mediums and sensitives.

The chakras form a chain of energy centres at which the etheric body interfaces with the physical body. In most Western systems there are said to be seven major chakras, root, sacral, solar plexus, heart, throat, brow and crown. These have connections to the major endocrine glands and the functions associated with them. The chakras are visualised as wheels vibrating at different frequencies with the root chakra having the lowest frequency and the crown having the highest.

It now appears that there are further chakras, one below our feet, in the ground, which maintains our connection with the earth and keeps us grounded, and others above our heads connecting with our soul and spirit aspects.

This is obviously a simplified approximation of the make-up of a human being and not everyone subscribes to quite the same scheme, or the same number of chakras. The truth is that we are unlikely to have the whole picture and different viewpoints can produce apparent discrepancies. However that may be, having such a scheme in mind adds to our understanding of the nature of health and disease and opens up great vistas of therapeutic possibilities.

It is reasonable to assume that higher vibrational frequencies are more powerful than lower ones and hence can influence them. It is believed that it is our spiritual aspects which determine the blueprint of our genes and genetic characteristics. Our spiritual aspirations, or lack of them, are therefore likely to affect profoundly our thoughts and emotions, and all of them can affect the physical body. Some physical problems and diseases are therefore likely to be a reflection of emotional or mental difficulties and blockages and also of our spiritual beliefs, manifesting at the physical level. From this point of view the idea that all health problems are purely physical and can be treated at that level is obviously absurd and is one reason why modern medicine is so often ineffective. We all know people who have been told that their complaints are all in the mind and therefore not real. Consequently their problems tend to be disregarded.

DIET AND NUTRITION

Our physical bodies are indeed composed of chemicals, the main elements being carbon, hydrogen, oxygen, nitrogen, phosphorus and sulphur, and a whole host of other minerals and trace elements. The primary building blocks of our cells and tissues are the carbohydrates, proteins and fats, which can be combined into mucopolysaccharides (protein and carbohydrate) and lipoproteins (protein and fat). Our cell membranes are largely protein and lipoprotein, and fatty compounds also figure largely in our brains and other nervous tissues. These structural molecules are built up by organised chains of biological catalysts, or enzymes, which are largely protein with vitamins and minerals at their active sites. The whole is a finely orchestrated network of biochemical reactions, dependent on the nervous system, enzymes, hormones and other messenger molecules to keep it functioning harmoniously. These processes are controlled by the inherited characteristics encoded in our genes. All this harmonious function is in turn dependent on the underlying electrical charges on the biological molecules, structural components and the genes themselves. Energy production and utilisation are also dependent on these biological charges in which trace elements and vitamins play an important part.

A nutritious diet must therefore contain adequate amounts of proteins and fats or oils, together with the necessary vitamins, minerals and trace elements, and some carbohydrate. Carbohydrate is not as important as protein or fat as it can be made from these, but protein cannot be made from carbohydrate. We are now discovering that there is also a whole spectrum of specialised biological compounds such as oligomeric proanthocyanidins (OPCs), quercetins, pycnogenols and other free radical scavengers/anti-oxidants, xanthones and lycopenes which are necessary for vibrant health. These essential dietary components come from plants in our diet.

Until about a century ago in this country food was organically produced, was largely unprocessed and still retained most of its vital nutrients when it arrived on the dining table. One of the earliest forms of processing, introduced in the nineteenth century, was the powerful steel roller mill which could remove all the bran from the grain and so produce refined white flour as opposed to the homely wholemeal variety. Refined in more ways than one.

Unfortunately this process removed the B-group vitamins, minerals, proteins and oils from the flour and paved the way for the recognition of vitamin deficiency diseases. It is only when we start refining, processing and adulterating food that we begin to realise that subtle, essential components have also been removed.

Today much of the food eaten by the majority of people has been processed into so-called convenience foods. The processing removes most of the essential nutrients from the food, the vitamins, minerals and other trace elements, and replaces them with a variety of chemicals, the flavourings and flavour enhancers, colourings, texturisers, stabilisers, emulsifiers and preservatives, none of which has been properly assessed for safety, particularly in combination. Add to this the chemicals, the pesticides, herbicides and artificial fertilisers that get into food while it is being grown and produced, and the use of sugar substitutes, most of which are probably more toxic than the sugar they are designed to replace, and it can readily be appreciated that food is often neither healthy nor nutritious. A lot of it actually makes us ill. The sugar substitute ASPARTAME in particular is highly toxic and now appears in almost all bottled drinks, whether they also contain sugar or not.

All this, of course, is a case of a lack of essential nutrients coupled with chemical additives making us ill, and it can be treated effectively by eating a whole food, fresh food, organically produced diet. Organic food is becoming easier to obtain these days, though it tends to be dearer than the more mass-produced, non-organic equivalents. In the interests of the health of the nation subsidies should be given to organic farmers and producers, not to those using artificial chemicals.

In this connection rock dust is important. The use of artificial fertilisers instead of natural manures and composts, coupled with overcropping, has reduced the trace mineral content of most of Planet Earth's soils to the extent that in 1992 Australia was best at only 55% DEPLETED, Europe and South America were 76% DEPLETED and the USA was 85% DEPLETED. It therefore comes as a surprise to learn that the World Health Organisation believes that we can get all the nutrients we require from our food, irrespective of how it is produced or the state of the soil. It must, however, be remembered that the WHO is merely another bureaucratic organisation manipulated by vested interests.

Rock dust is the ground up volcanic rock deposited by glaciers, unleached of its minerals, Added to the soil, it restores the mineral and trace element content of the soil allowing luxurious growth and nutritional excellence of the plants grown on it. Rock dust contains high concentrations of calcium and magnesium which, on exposure to the air, can take up carbon dioxide to form the appropriate carbonates. If used on a large scale world-wide, this could help to counteract global warming appreciably.

The dietary advice I give is to buy fresh, unprocessed whole food, organically grown if possible, and cook it yourself. This will cut down considerably on the unwanted chemicals which are ingested. It is also a good idea to eat from as many different food groups and sources as you can. Different plant species synthesise different biologically important compounds. Humankind evolved eating from a very wide variety of different foods and their different biological components became important for keeping us in vibrant good health.

Avoid junk foods, processed foods, bottled drinks and all chemical additives where possible. It is also a good idea to avoid the "heavy" concentrated carbohydrates, the grains and especially, wheat – and this includes pasta and pizza as well as bread and other bakery products – potatoes and sugar, but please avoid the sugar substitutes. A little sugar, especially unrefined sugar, or honey is preferable to the substitutes. It is the heavy carbohydrates, especially if processed, e.g. white flour and white sugar, which increase our weight, cholesterol and blood pressure. Low fat and particularly no fat diets are unhealthy as we need fats and oils to build our bodies and provide the fat soluble vitamins A and D. Butter, cream, olive oil, seeds, nuts and avocados, together with the oily fish, are the healthiest sources of fat or oil. Peanuts are not nuts, they are a pulse and can cause allergies. Soya, another pulse, is also increasingly becoming involved in allergy production.

ENERGY FIELDS

Underlying the physical body which we can see and perceive, is our biochemical structure, the vast and intricate network of biological processes which digest and assimilate our food, maintain our structure, produce our energy, protect us from infections and other harmful outside influences, repair any damage, mediate our reproduction and clear out all the harmful and toxic wastes which these many chemical processes generate. It is at our biochemical level that good nutrition, vitamins, minerals and trace elements (many of which are co-factors for the enzymes) play their very important role. From this point of view the body IS a complex series of chemical reactions.

However, behind the biochemistry is the level of the atoms and sub-atomic particles with their positive and negative charges, which are the important mediators of all chemical and biochemical reactions. This brings us into the realms of our energy fields which are part of the electro-magnetic spectrum. The higher the frequency of vibration of a substance, the finer and less dense it is, and beyond a certain frequency range, the human senses are unable to detect it. It is therefore considered not to exist.

We can measure the electrical activity of our muscles, hearts and brains, but we cannot see these energies any more than we can see electricity. We know that electricity exists because we have instruments that detect it and by the effects that it produces. We can detect changes in brain waves in certain forms of brain activity but we do not know how these are translated into our thoughts and actions, nor can we detect what really underlies our emotions. Our emotional and mental levels are thus largely ignored by orthodox medicine although very much a part of some aspects of complementary medicine.

An appreciation of the importance of the mental and emotional aspects of humanity underlies much of complementary medicine in areas such as homœopathy. flower essences, psychotherapy, neurolinguistic programming (NLP), thought field therapy, Bowen Therapy and so on. This appreciation enlarges the scope for treatment enormously and gives complementary medicine a decisive edge over orthodox, drug based treatments which are often inappropriate. Energy field rebalancing techniques such as acupuncture, shiatsu, reiki, bioenergy/biaura and computerised bioresonance techniques all come into this category and can all be used successfully to treat many conditions which are beyond the scope of pharmaceutical medicine.

Thought field therapy (TFT), developed by Roger Callaghan in the 1980s is a further extension of the therapeutic possibilities inherent in the appreciation of the importance of the emotional and mental aspects of the human being. It eliminates perturbations in the thought fields by tapping specific points on the body in a specific sequence and can be used for the rapid reversal of problems such as addictions, obsession, phobias, traumas and post traumatic stress syndrome, grief, guilt, rejection, anxiety, panic disorders, self sabotage, depression and many other painful emotional/mental conditions. Homoeopathy and the Australian Bush Flower essences can also address these mental and emotional problems. It is likely that most, if not all flower essences can be helpful here but my main experience is with the Australian ones.

WATER FLUORIDATION

The topics considered up till now have tended to take a wide view of the living body, its health and disease. Even nutrition and the idea of supplementing essential nutrients no longer freely available from the diet, take a broader view than many pharmaceutically trained physicians today. One is still often met with the comment "what's all this nonsense about diet" though this is beginning to change. The tendency is still to think that chemicals can sort out everything.

This conflict between diet and lifestyle on the one hand and chemical approaches on the other is shown up very clearly by the water fluoridation controversy. The main causes of tooth decay are eating too many sweets and other sugary foods and neglecting to clean the teeth. It has nothing to do with a perceived "lack" of fluoride in the diet. There is no such thing as a fluoride deficient diet and there never has been. Fluoride is NOT an essential component of a healthy diet and it is NOT an essential component of our bodies. It is NOT a nutrient. On the contrary, it is one of the most toxic substances found in the earth's crust. It is classified as a Part II poison which means that technically it is a criminal offence to put it into anybody's water supply.

However, the idea that fluoride helps to prevent tooth decay is supported by powerful business interests, the sugar industry, phosphate fertiliser manufacturing and other fluoride producing industries. When it was realised that aluminium smelting, phosphate fertiliser manufacturing and a host of other industries produced hydrogen fluoride gas which was allowed to escape up the factory chimneys and that this was causing widespread destructive effects on vegetation, domestic animals and wildlife which ate the fluoride polluted grass, legislation was enacted whereby scrubbers had to be installed in the factory chimneys to remove the hydrogen fluoride gas. This was trapped in silica compounds, forming sodium hydrofluorosilicates and hydrofluorosilicic acid, both of which are highly toxic, and are known in the trade as pollution scrubber liquor. This is contaminated with lead, mercury, beryllium, antimony and radionucleides some of which are known carcinogens. This caused a problem for the fluoride producers because it was both expensive and difficult to dispose of it.

When it was noted that in some areas of Texas people had teeth which, although stained and mottled, were resistant to decay, and it was also discovered that their water supplies contained fluoride compounds naturally, this was hailed as a life-saver for the fluoride producers. They could dispose of their toxic wastes AND protect teeth at the same time. What they failed to notice was that the fluoride-containing waters also contained a spectrum of trace minerals such as calcium, magnesium, manganese, zinc, copper, cobalt, selenium, chromium and vanadium, and that it was these minerals, and not the fluoride, that protect the teeth and incidentally help to protect the rest of the body against the ravages of the fluoride compounds. Where such trace minerals do not occur in naturally fluoridated waters, as in areas of the Punjab, the population suffers from devastating skeletal and dental fluorosis.

Fluoride is a powerful inhibitor of many enzyme systems and related metabolic processes in the body. Far from protecting teeth, it actually destroys them, disrupting the structure of the enamel, making it hard but brittle, leading to dental fluorosis which can occur in all degrees from very mild to total destruction of the teeth. It is highly disfiguring and has an enormous emotional and social impact on those suffering from it. A recent review found that in fluoridated areas up to 48% of the population suffered from dental fluorosis in one degree or another. It is extremely expensive to disguise, requiring repeated capping of the teeth, and this treatment is not available on the NHS, even although it has been caused by Government decree.

Dental fluorosis is the first VISIBLE sign of fluoride poisoning. Fluoride also affects the bones causing skeletal fluorosis, the thyroid gland causing hypothyroidism, the pancreas, the brain, liver, kidneys, stomach, immune system and even our chromosomes and genes. The damaging effects of fluoride on health are disastrous. At the moment, because of the 7-fold increase in osteosarcoma in young men, many powerful organisations in the US, including the 7,000 scientists at the

US Environmental Protection Agency, are seeking to have the fluorides used in water fluoridation classified as carcinogens. Yet this public health measure was conceived politically as a chemical way to sort out diet and lifestyle. It also saves the fluoride producers untold millions of dollars annually as well as bringing in income from fluoridated toothpaste, drops, dental floss, dental filling materials and other dental products. Not surprisingly, the toxic effects of water fluoridation are vehemently denied by the vested interests involved, and have been for over fifty years.

PHARMACEUTICAL DRUGS

The mistaken idea that chemicals can be an answer to most ill-health and disease situations also underpins the drug industry and the big multinational pharmaceutical corporations, collectively referred to in many quarters as Big Pharma. The pharmaceutical industry is a mega million dollar industry world wide and it has a virtual stranglehold on health and disease at this time. It has been truly said that "he who produces the treatment controls the disease".

During the course of the last century, and particularly since the end of the Second World War, we have seen the emergence of major epidemics of chronic degenerative diseases. Whereas in previous centuries, and into the twentieth, infectious diseases were the major scourges, since about the mid 1950s and onwards we have witnessed rapidly increasing prevalences of heart disease and strokes, high blood pressure, abdominal problems, arthritis, allergies, obesity, neurological problems and cancer. Where a century ago these conditions were rare, now at least one quarter of children have asthma requiring inhalers and it seems that two out of three people will develop cancer. A recent study suggests that 60% of the WORLD'S population now suffers from chronic degenerative disease. If certain advertisements are to be believed, two out of three people have a raised blood cholesterol, whatever that may mean. The upper limits of normal of both cholesterol and blood pressure are continually being revised downwards. The cynical among us suspect that this reflects a growing need for Big Pharma to sell more drugs, and make obscenely bigger and bigger profits, rather than a true increase in ill-health.

Whatever may be the truth of this, Big Pharma rides to the rescue with treatments for all of these chronic degenerative diseases in the belief that they can all be sorted out with more synthetic chemicals.

There are two major problems with this approach.

The first is that they do not conduct any valid scientific research to discover why these diseases are becoming so rampant. They take the explanation that best suits their purposes and then proceed to manufacture drugs to counteract the symptoms and signs of the disease.

The second mistake is to believe that yet another set of synthetic, body-unfriendly chemicals will effectively address conditions many of which have been caused in the first place by poor diet and chemicals of one sort or another. By their very nature all pharmaceutical drugs have side-effects, but this suits Big Pharma rather well because it can then offer another range of pharmaceuticals to off-set the side effects of the first lot, and so on. We all know people who have virtually become their own private chemists' shops without any noticeable improvement in their health and well-being.

The major causes of the chronic degenerative diseases are dietary and/or environmental.

A lack of essential nutrients, the vitamins, minerals, trace elements and other natural essential biological compounds is a prime cause of much of the ill-health seen today. As mentioned earlier, these essential biological components of our diet and of our bodies are integral parts of our metabolism. Without them our bodies do not function optimally, and tissue repair, energy production, immune system function and so on, begin to break down, causing the body to be not at ease and hence dis-eased and then diseased. Much of this damage, if caught early enough, can be repaired effectively by giving a wide spectrum of vitamins, minerals and trace elements. Since we do not really know the bodily requirements of any of these nutrients, which vary widely from individual to individual, and since they do not work in isolation, but synergistically, it is best to give a spread of both vitamins and minerals and let the body select what it needs. Overdosing is unlikely, especially if the person is deficient in the first place.

Another important problem with diet is the misinformation with which we are bombarded. We are told the carbohydrates are good, that fats are bad causing overweight and high cholesterol levels, and that we should not eat too much protein. It seems to have been forgotten that our food must provide us with the materials necessary to repair and maintain our bodies, as well as providing us with energy. We are constructed from protein and fat or oil, along with a number of minerals, trace elements and vitamins. Carbohydrate can be made easily from protein and is not required in any great amount.

In the past twenty years or so, and now with increasing rapidity, people have been becoming more and more obese. Often it is not that they are eating too much, but that they are eating the wrong foods, Carbohydrate burns in a fire of fat. In order to burn carbohydrate fuel for energy, we require some fat. Fat reduced and fat-free diets are therefore distinctly unhealthy and further predispose to obesity. It is not fat that makes us fat, as the food manufacturers would have us believe, but heavy carbohydrates, particularly the devitalised, processed forms. Probably about one third protein, one third fat and one third carbohydrate would be about right for most people, but if people have a lot of weight to lose, they need to cut out all heavy carbohydrates, that is, sugar, the grains and all their products, bread, pasta, pizza etc., and potatoes, and concentrate on protein foods with their attendant fats and oils, salads, green vegetables, seeds and nuts, and not too many root vegetables. Remember that peanuts are NOT nuts. Anyone who is now obese has stopped burning carbohydrates years ago, or they would not be that way. The carbohydrates which they eat just end up in the fat stores making the problem increasingly worse. The body has to be carbohydrate deprived to force it into burning the fat stores. The Atkins diet is about the best there is for dealing with this situation, but it is vehemently hated by the food manufacturers since it cuts out all the processed rubbish foods and concentrates instead on real food bought whole and fresh, and organically produced if possible. Another series of chemicals, as manufactured by Big Pharma, will NEVER cure obesity.

Excess carbohydrate in the diet, especially wheat which seems to be associated with a pesticide or altered pesticide residue carry over, can also cause raised cholesterol and blood pressure, heart attacks, strokes and diabetes. Most of the cholesterol in the body is produced by the body itself. It is the starting material for all our steroid hormones, which mediate our carbohydrate metabolism, salt and water balance, our ability to cope with stress and our sexual function. Cholesterol is an essential component of our bodies. Lower it too much and you die. It is likely that in most cases, a rise in cholesterol levels is an effect of pesticides or other chemicals inhibiting the breakdown and disposal of cholesterol, not an excessive intake. It has to be remembered that these days the food manufacturing giants and Big Pharma are all part of the same commercial conglomerate. From a business point of view, this is an excellent position because if they make you ill with their food, or other chemicals, they can then suggest some of Big Pharma's remedies. They are laughing all the way to the bank but the health effects are devastating. It is not surprising that the National Health Service is so crippled. It tries to cope with the destructive effects of diet while at the same time being virtually run by the drug companies.

HRT AND NATURAL PROGESTERONE.

I hope that by now it is becoming apparent that there are sensible, natural, inexpensive and non-toxic solutions to most of the health problems we face today. Another case in point is hormone replacement therapy, HRT.

Menopause in women is a natural occurrence, the point at which a woman becomes free from the menstrual cycle and the "risk" of pregnancy, and becomes a much freer agent in her own right. In primitive societies women often came into their power after menopause, becoming the revered healers and wise women of the tribe. Today menopause tends to be thought of as a disease. Why? Because we have HRT, don't we? Remember he who makes the treatment controls the disease.

Prior to the twentieth century, menopausal symptoms do not seem to have been a problem and women did not suffer from osteoporosis in the way they seem to today. Even now many women, probably over 50%, do not suffer menopausal problems. When a seventeenth century graveyard was discovered in London a few years ago when foundations were being dug for a new high-rise building, it was noted that none of the skeletons showed signs of osteoporosis even though some were from women in their seventies or older.

Prior to the middle of the twentieth century, pesticides and other biocides were not used in agriculture, and although there was processed food, it did not form such a large part of the average diet as it does now. Overall nutrition was better than it is now.

Pesticides, herbicides, petrochemicals and a host of other industrial solvents and chemicals are oestrogen mimics, that is, they are xeno-oestrogens, substances foreign to the body which can exert an oestrogen effect. Excess oestrogen or oestrogen effect suppresses ovulation around the middle of the menstrual cycle and therefore impairs the production of progesterone in the second half of the cycle. Since oestrogen and progesterone balance each other, an increasing tendency to oestrogen dominance develops. The symptoms of premenstrual syndrome/tension (PMS or PMT) are largely the symptoms of unopposed oestrogen, that is, oestrogen not balanced by progesterone. Dr. John Lee in California reckoned that many women after the age of thirty five no longer ovulated regularly, although they could continue to have regular periods for a further fifteen years, that is until about age fifty. They therefore became increasingly oestrogen dominant and suffered from hot flushes and sweats, breast tenderness and swelling, fluid retention, weight gain and mood swings, the symptoms of unopposed oestrogen. At menopause when the oestrogen levels drop by some 40-60%, the symptoms may ameliorate, but the state of oestrogen dominance continues.

The drug companies' answer is HRT, mainly oestrogen, usually synthetic, though this can sometimes be combined with a synthetic progestogen (called progestin in the US), combined HRT. More oestrogen is NOT what is required although it must be admitted that it does seem to improve the symptoms in some women for a while. Progestogens do not have the beneficial effects of natural progesterone and have their own array of side-effects and contraindications. Many women on HRT just do not feel well. It is now established that HRT can predispose to heart attacks, strokes, deep venous thrombosis and breast cancer. The contraceptive pill is, of course, oestrogen, sometimes combined with progestogen. This is often prescribed to girls in their teens for menstrual difficulties as well as for contraception. The long-term effects of this on cancer incidence have yet to be evaluated. Despite this, Big Pharma continues to push its HRT to the consternation of at least SOME of the medical profession.

Natural progesterone, which is the missing hormone, does not have any side-effects. It is required for the maintenance of pregnancy and if there is insufficient miscarriage often results. If progesterone had any adverse effects no normal babies, either human or of any other mammalian species, would ever have been born.

Natural progesterone is therefore safe to use both before and after menopause. It prevents and cures the symptoms of PMS and menopause, protects against and treats osteoporosis, protects against breast cancer, protects the heart and is an immune system enhancer. It improves energy levels and is a mood elevator. As one patient said "it puts the icing back on your gingerbread" Another stated that "joie de vivre has returned". Big Pharma, however, will not countenance it and even tries to blame the side effects of progestogens on progesterone. It is, after all, a competitor for HRT. However, as in many other areas, synthetic pharmaceuticals will not, long term, substitute for the natural remedy.

VACCINATION PROGRAMMES

This is another area in which Big Pharma is deeply involved.

In the UK the idea started with Dr. Edward Jenner at the end of the eighteenth centrury. He had observed that milkmaids who were exposed to cowpox from their cows did not normally develop smallpox, which was, and still is, a serious infectious disease. He developed the idea that if people were given the mild disease cowpox, it would protect them from the ravages of smallpox. The term vaccination comes from the Latin vacca, a cow, since it was the cowpox pustules on the cows that were used to "vaccinate" people.

As this approach proved to be successful, the idea was gradually extended to other infectious diseases once the infecting agents had been identified. Two approaches were developed.

1. Passive immunisation which involved the injection of serum from someone who had recovered from the disease, into another person to prevent the disease or treat early cases of it. This approach is not long lasting but is useful in an emergency.

2. The second approach is to inject the infecting agent in a killed or attenuated form into a person to stimulate them to produce their own immunity. In theory this provides longer lasting protection.

This idea had a great appeal in the early twentieth century when infectious diseases were much more of a scourge than they are now, in the Western world at least. It was thought that by vaccinating/immunising children to the infectious diseases, these would be wiped out and a herd immunity established.

Unfortunately theory does not always translate well into practice and today we have more and more children being vaccinated to more and more infectious diseases without any apparent end in sight. What has gone wrong here?

There are a number of serious flaws in the theory as it is practised. In the first place, when babies are born their immune systems are still immature and they do not start to become immunocompetent until sometime after six months of age and their immune systems are unlikely to be fully functional until they are about four years old. Nature intended this vulnerable period at the start of life to be covered by passive immunisation passed on from the mother in her milk. Unfortunately, if the mother does not breast feed, the infant misses out on this protection. Ideally breast feeding should be continued until at least six to nine months by which time the baby's immune system is better able to cope.

Secondly, when we get an infection naturally, we just get one at a time. The body is therefore able to direct its defences towards just one agent. Originally single preparations were used in the vaccination schedules and vaccinations did not start until the age of six to nine months. However, with the introduction of vaccinations to more and more diseases, single preparations would entail too many injections for the poor baby, too many visits to the GPs' surgeries and too much time taken. The tendency has therefore been to combine inocculations to several different diseases into one jab, hence we have MMR (measles, mumps and rubella {German measles}), DPT (diphtheria, pertussus {whooping cough} and tetanus) with more combinations in the pipeline. Also, in order to get all the vaccinations in, the injections now start at two months or earlier, and are repeated at four months and six months. Often MMR, DPT and polio are all given at the same time, which makes seven diseases to be coped with at once by a baby whose immune system is incapable of handling this. It is not surprising that the success rate of such programmes is low and that the injections have to be continually repeated.

3. A further flaw lies in the fact that the wrong route is used for the administration of the vaccines. When we contract an infectious disease the usual route of infection is by droplets inhaled through the nose or mouth, from an infected person sneezing or coughing. This ensures that a full immune response is mounted since the immune complex IgA is produced by the mucous membranes lining our noses,

throats and respiratory tracts, and IgG later when the infectious agent penetrates the blood stream. IgG is considered to be less protective than IgA. Injections bipass the mucous membranes and therefore IgA is not produced; only IgG. Thus at best only partial immunity can be achieved.

Fourthly, as if all this were not bad enough, modern vaccines contain preservatives, often mercury based, adjuvants to enhance the response and foreign proteins derived from the culture medium used to grow the organism being used. All of these can be toxic, particularly to babies and young children, and foreign proteins induce allergies in their own right. Mercury is known to affect the brain. It is suspected that much of the phenomenal rise in the number of allergy sufferers may be related to vaccinations.

The infectious diseases of childhood are developmental diseases, conferring benefits on the development and maturation of the growing child. Measles for instance, strengthens the blood-brain barrier and whooping cough strengthens the lungs. The gradual exposure to these diseases, one at a time, exercises and strengthens the immune system. There is growing concern in some quarters that the vaccination programmes, far from preventing disease, are actually laying us open to new or altered and more insidious diseases. They do not reliably prevent infection by the infectious agents, but they suppress the rashes and make the infections difficult to diagnose. The rashes are actually a part of the healing response and when they erupt the sufferer often feels better. By suppressing the rashes, vaccination modifies the condition and turns it in to deeper levels where it may predispose to cancer such as Hodgkin's Disease or autoimmune disease later in life.

The protection afforded by vaccination has been found to be short-lived, much shorter and less effective than immunity acquired by contracting the disease naturally. Injections therefore have to be repeated throughout childhood, but this leaves the adult population relatively unprotected, and these diseases are more serious if acquired in adulthood rather than in childhood.

There are growing concerns that current vaccination programmes are undermining the immune systems of our children, leaving them vulnerable to many infections and predisposing in no small measure to the growing incidence of allergies and other chronic diseases. When the immune systems of populations are undermined, whether by vaccinations, environmental pollution or vitamin and mineral deficiencies, they are more likely to fall prey to pandemics such as the Asian bird flu or SARS virus.

Big Pharma has a large vested interest in the vaccination programmes. This became apparent when it was suggested that all children in Scotland should be vaccinated against measles even if they had actually had measles. Andrew Wakefield's controversial research suggests that measles vaccination can lead to autism and this was very disturbing to Big Pharma. It is illogical to vaccinate anyone who has already had the disease since the natural disease produces a far better immunity.

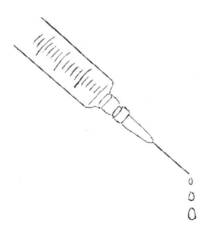

OTHER AREAS OF CONCERN
TRANSPLANT SURGERY

Transplant surgery has been hailed as a great boon and blessing to man. Certainly the technical expertise and skill required are impressive, but this approach is, once again, treating the individual like a machine to have spare parts replaced as required.

It is impossible to get a complete tissue match so a compromise has to be reached with heavy suppression of the recipient's immune system to prevent rejection of the transplant. Rejection occurs when the body mounts an immune response to the foreign proteins in the transplant, but since the immune system is also our protection and repair apparatus, its suppression leaves the recipient vulnerable to developing severe infections and even possibly cancer, should he/she live that long.

The need for transplants, mainly hearts and kidneys, is usually the result of lifestyle faults, particularly, once again, the diet. If these predisposing factors were addressed sufficiently early there would be no need for transplant surgery with all its attendant dangers. If, however, a transplant is carried out again treating symptoms rather than the cause, then if appropriate dietary and other lifestyle changes are not made, the new organ will suffer the same fate as its predecessor and will gradually become as diseased as the organ which it replaced.

There are also concerns in some quarters about the effects that someone else's organ may have on the recipient. Does the organ carry information about the mental and emotional status of the donor? Could this affect the recipient? What might be the effect on the donor, whether alive or dead, of having part of their physical body walking around in someone else? Since transplant surgery is part of the purely materialistic way of thinking about people, such possibilities are not considered and certainly not investigated. I know of one woman who developed an allergy to wine after a cataract transplant. Presumably the donor had an allergy to wine. The effects of the mental, emotional and spiritual components of a transplant are not even considered as a possibility. How much better it would be if lifestyle faults could be corrected before transplantation becomes necessary.

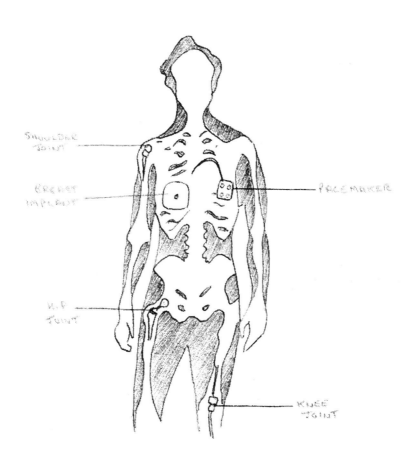

GENETIC MODIFICATION.

Transplant surgery is confined to the macroscopic elements of the body but genetic engineering, or genetic modification goes much deeper. Our genetic code is very delicately balanced and we really do not know how one section of it modifies another. There are large sections of our genome which apparently have no function, but this is very unlikely to be the case since nature does not countenance waste. Our genes are sensitive to even minor changes. Many inherited metabolic diseases such as phenylketonuria, galactosæmia or hæmophilia, are the result of just one change in the whole length of a gene, known as a point mutation. Such an apparently minor change can have devastating results as in the diseases just mentioned, while in other cases it may be harmless or even beneficial.

Genetic engineering and genetic modification were developed as a means for big business to patent natural substances, which by definition cannot be patented or owned commercially. However, it was realised that if certain organisms or plants were genetically modified or engineered, they could no longer be considered to be natural and would be the property of those who produced them. It reduces them to the status of the pharmaceutical drugs and is a backdoor way to exploiting and controlling the natural world in a truly fundamental manner. If extended as the genetic engineering companies would like to see, it would, and does, put enormous power and financial resources into the hands of just a few individuals, reducing most of the rest of the world to the status of slaves. These companies would like to own the human genome – after all, what is the human genome mapping project really all about? It is very unlikely to be for the good of our health and the eradication of genetic diseases, as we are led to believe.

There are major problems with genetic modification and genetic engineering. In the first place it is very imprecise since the genetic scientists cannot accurately control where the added or modified genes will enter the DNA chain, the building block of our genes. As already mentioned, even one mistake in the coding, or one deletion at the modified site could have effects which range from no obvious impairment to profound and severe changes and even death of the organism. There is no way that the genetic scientists can avoid with certainty such situations from occuring when they carry out their so-called modifications, and there is no way that they can foretell what other effects such modifications may have. Unpredictable results probaby occur far oftener than we are allowed to know. For instance when the gene for cold resistance from flounders was introduced into salmon, the salmon grew ten times as fast as ordinary salmon because the inserted gene interfered with their growth hormone gene.

An example which was highly publicised at the time was the effect of a batch of genetically modified L-tryptophan, a naturally occuring amino acid and a vital component of our bodies, in causing serious blood disorders in thousands of people in the US, of whom more than thirty died. Unfortunately these side-effects were blamed on the L-tryptophan, which of course was nonsense since it is an essential component of ourselves. It was however banned in the interests of safety (or someone else's commercial interests maybe) while the true culprit, genetic modification, escaped unblamed - by the authorities.

Allergies can also be transferred along with modified genes. People who have allergies to nuts, for instance, have been known to become allergic to products such as soya which was modified with genes from nuts.

Genes for modification are often spliced into the recipient organism using viruses as the carrier and these carry their own inherent risks. It has also been found that genetically modified plants such as potatoes and oil seed rape can pollinate unmodified plants more than a mile away. Once the modified genes have invaded the environment in this way it is impossible to stop, or control the process. The future risks to the environment are impossible to assess and are likely to escalate, particularly if the modified varieties have an advantage over the natural plants. No-one can know the damage that may occur. We have to realise that these potential environmental and health risks are being imposed on the whole planet in the name of greed.

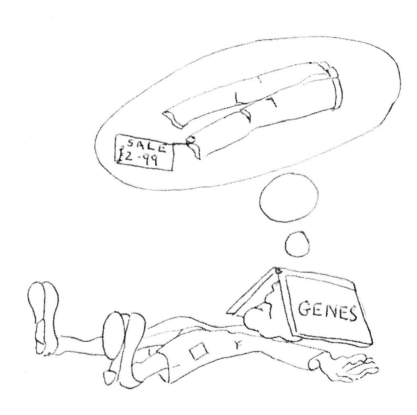

THE EUROPEAN UNION.

Orthodox medicine largely denies the importance of the mental, emotional and spiritual aspects of the human being, reducing us to a state of no hope if its chemical treatments fail us, as they do. The human being and the concepts of health and disease are reduced to the level of chemistry, a purely mechanistic viewpoint in which symptoms and signs are considered to be the disease and treatment is aimed at their suppression or elimination. Little consideration is given to why the condition has arisen in the first place, and if the condition is not amenable to treatment by drugs, there is little that modem medicine can do. Patients are not listened to, emotional, mental and subconscious aspects are not considered and if chemical treatments do not work, patients are told that they are just imagining their symptoms, or it is all in the mind and that is that. It is not real. The orthodox pharmaceuticals add their own burden of ill-health since all are potentially toxic. It is no surprise that the health of the nation continues to decline and the NHS itself is crumbling to its knees.

This situation is mirrored by the European Union, the EU, with its rigid bureaucratic structure and erosion of most, if not all, of our hard won rights and freedoms. If Britain fully joined the EU we would lose the power to determine our own future nationally, legally and economically, and be reduced to the status of a mere province of the European super-power. In Britain people are considered innocent until proved guilty but under European law all are guilty until proved innocent, and the European judges can decide, quite arbitrarily, and without trial by jury, whether someone is guilty or innocent. The EU has drained the British economy of more than £180 billion since we joined it. It is no wonder that we cannot afford to maintain our postal services, transport systems and education and is another reason why the health service is in such dire straits.

The EU is ruled by an unelected, unaccountable quango of bureaucrats who are greedy, dictatorial and corrupt. Billions of Euros have disappeared into a great black hole, never to be seen again. They certainly do not benefit the peoples of Europe. The EUs financial accounts have NEVER been published because the auditors have consistently refused to sign them.

The EU wishes to impose uniformity on us all and reduce all to the lowest common denominator. It seeks to regulate and control all aspects of our lives. Currently it is attempting to restrict our free access to vitamins, minerals, trace elements, food supplements and other healthy components of a balanced diet, and to ban many of them in the interests of uniformity (and big business, i.e. drug company, interests). Everyone is different, we all have differing needs, and therefore it is nonsense to try and impose uniformity. Similarly it is ludicrous to try to impose a common agricultural policy all the way from Scandinavia to the Mediterranean. This simply leads to misery and suffering for many. The important dietary supplements are the very things that help to protect us from the onslaught of environmental pollution, soil degradation, pharmaceutical drugs, vaccines and water fluoridation, but of course if many of us did not have these supplements we might be much more ill than we are, and might have to resort to the only things that will be left, the toxic pharmaceutical drugs.

We have to get right out of the European Union if we are to have any future worth having, and then re-negotiate the spirit of a caring, sharing community, each with our own national identity, rights and freedoms, laws and constitutions. This is NOT the agenda of the EU and its Council of Ministers as currently formulated. This fact was underlined by Giscard d'Estaing in May 2003 when he stated "Our constitution (i.e. The EU constitution) cannot be reduced to a mere treaty for co-operation between governments. Anyone who has not yet grasped this fact deserves to wear the dunce's cap". Such an agenda has to be opposed.

TOWARDS A HEALTHIER FUTURE
TAKE CHARGE OF YOUR BODY

The solutions to our current environmental and health problems are in essence simple, non-invasive, non-toxic, inexpensive and low tech, and could be implemented by any nation whether rich or poor. Such solutions, however, are opposed by the powerful vested interests of greed and corruption. One wonders if, in the aftermath of two devastating hurricanes, America (Bush) may yet sign up to the Kyoto Treaty.

Attention must first be directed towards diet and nutrition, considered by orthodoxy to be of little importance. The World Health Organisation believes that we can get all the nutrients we need from our food, irrespective of how it is produced, or the state of the soil, and the EU, as we have seen, is attempting to restrict and regulate our access to nutritional supplements. Improving our diet involves our agriculture and horticulture and other aspects of food production. Artificial fertilisers should be phased out along with pesticides, herbicides and other biocides, wherever possible. Manures, composts and rock dusts will help to restore soil fertility and balance and provide more nutritious food for the people. Even in a single growing season the application of rock dust to the soil can substantially increase the mineral and trace element contents of the food grown on it. All these measures would, of course, be violently opposed by the chemical companies.

The whole spectrum of reputable preparations of the vitamins, minerals, trace elements and other food supplements should remain freely available to all, as they are at present in the UK, and should not be banned or restricted by dictatorial EU regulations and vested interests which do not like competition in the market place. All people have a right to fresh, unprocessed, nutritious food and clean water unpolluted by fluoride and other noxious substances.

It is best if food is produced and consumed locally. This means that it is fresher when bought, and much transportation becomes unnecessary, potentially reducing the release of greenhouse gases to the environment.

Natural remedies and natural therapies can treat the health problems of humanity every bit as successfully, if not more so, than pharmaceutical drugs. They have the advantages of being largely free from side-effects and of being relatively inexpensive. They work in harmony with the body, not against it, as is the case with orthodox pharmaceuticals, and can actually help the body to heal. It tends to be forgotten that the body is naturally a self-healing organism, given half a chance and, if necessary, a helping hand.

Homœopathy, flower essences and herbal remedies are reputable, well tried and tested methods of treatment whatever the orthodox fraternity and those who like to talk about "evidence based medicine" might like to say. If they were serious about evidence based they would realise that methods which have successfully treated people for hundreds of years are certainly evidence based. Of course the vested interests of the drug companies wish to suppress these natural treatment methods, hence the scathing attacks.

Both homœopathy and the flower essences have the ability to address emotional and mental problems as well as physical complaints. The flower remedies from the Australian Bush are remarkably successful in dealing with the whole range of psychological problems more safely and effectively than any psychologist or psychiatrist.

However help for the psychological aspects of ill-health is not confined to these. Talking things over with friends and family, hypnotherapy, neurolinguistic programming (NLP), thought field therapy (TFT) and other related treatments can all be remarkably powerful and successful in dealing with emotional crises, addiction, phobias, stress and post traumatic stress syndrome. It is not necessary to have the patient re-experience the traumatic event for healing to occur. It can be done safely, quickly, effectively and enjoyably and it is a pity that these approaches are not more widely recognised and used.

When it comes to more physical complaints such as sore backs, muscle aches and pains. arthritis (which is also amenable to natural therapies such as homoeopathy and the New Zealand green lipped mussel), frozen shoulders, whip-lash injuries, tennis elbows, carpal tunnel syndrome, lumbago, sciatica and so on, therapies such as massage, aromatherapy, acupuncture, reflexology, shiatsu, reiki, craniosacral therapy, Bowen therapy, cervical reintegration and other muscle-relaxing techniques, and energy balancing techniques such as bioresonance and bioenergy/biaura can be very successful.

There are many different techniques to chose from and some suit some people better than others. All are non-toxic and relatively non-invasive and apart from the computerised bioresonance programmes, are low tech and inexpensive compared with pharmaceutical drugs, transplants and so on. They are affordable and although some are relatively time consuming, many are not, effecting considerable relief within the course of half an hour or less.

What stops many of the wonderful complementary therapies from being more widely practised and therefore more widely available is the scorn and derision of orthodoxy which hates to be upstaged and shown to be wanting. Vested interests as embodied, for instance, in the EU, would like to stamp out all these gentle, kindly, inexpensive, effective techniques in the interests of egotism, greed and power.

Many in the complementary field would like to see their complementary techniques and therapies becoming the main treatment methods. If this were to occur, we must still remain vigilant because it would be only too easy for the orthodox big business conglomerates to usurp them and then proceed to curtail, regulate and control them from within, for their own ends. This would have to be resisted at all costs.

These wonderful therapies should be practised from a state of higher wisdom, compassion and caring and should be available to all. The idea of exploiting everything to make money, as seems to be swamping the world at present, must be abandoned if we and our planet, and all our brothers and sisters in the animal and plant kingdoms are to survive and prosper. If greed, vested interests and ego trips were kept out of the picture, everyone would be able to enjoy better, vibrant health and happiness. It is iniquitous that peoples' distress and suffering should be turned into an opportunity to make millions of pounds or dollars. Big Pharma, the chemical companies and the food manufacturers have a lot for which to answer.

This little book is not intended to be an encyclopaedia of complementary medicine. It is intended as a wake-up call to lay people and professionals alike. It is up to us all to make conscious changes to our life-styles to improve our health and happiness, remembering that man does not live by bread alone. It is time that we put less emphasis on the material side of life and a bit more on the higher, spiritual values. That way lies true health and happiness.

RESOURCES

Atkins Diet
Atkins Nutritionals Inc.
2002 Orville Drive North,
Suite A,
Ronkonkoma,
NY 11779-7661,
USA.
www.atkinscenter.com

Australian Bush Essences
46 Booralie Road,
Terry Hills,
New South Wales, 2084,
Australia
info@ausflowers.com.au
www.ausflowers.com.au

Bi-Aura Foundation,
Newton,
Stocksfield,
Northumberland
NE4S 7UN
Tel.   01661 844 899
info@bi-aura.com

BioCare Ltd.   Vitamins and mineral supplements
Lakeside,
180 Lifford Lane,
Kings Norton,
Birmingham
B30 3NU
Tel. 0121 433 3727.
biocare@biocare.co.uk

Bowtech (Bowen Therapy Association of Australia).
The Bowen Association of the United Kingdom
PO Box 4358,
Dorchester,
Dorset
DT1 3BA
Tel. 0700 269 8324.
office@bowen-technique.co.uk
www.bowen-technique.co.uk

Campaign for an Independent Britain,
81 Ashmole Street,
London
SW8 1NF
Tel. 020 8340 0314
info@cibhq.co.uk
http://www.cibhq.co.uk

Campaign to reject the European Constitution (CREC)
32 Station Road,
Poppleton,
York
Y026 6PY
Tel. 01904 795 204.
graham.wood32@tiscali.co.uk
www.european-constitution.org.uk

Faculty of Homœopathy,
Hahnemann House,
29 Park Street West,
Luton
LU1 3BE.
Tel. 0870 444 3955.
info@trusthomeopathy.org
www.trusthomeopathy.org/faculty

International Flower Essence Repertoire,
Achamore House,
Isle of Gigha,
Argyll
PA41 7AD
Tel. 01583 505 385
gigha@atlas.co.uk
www.healingflowers.com

Higher Nature Plc.   Vitamins, minerals, food supplements,
Burwash Common,
East Sussex
TN19 7LX.
Tel   01435 882 880.

Nature's Own/Cytoplan   Vitamins, minerals, food supplements,
Unit 8 Hanley Workshops,
Hanley Swan,
Worcestershire
WT8 ODX.
Tel. 01684 310 099.
sales@cytoplan.co.uk
www.cytoplan.co.uk

Rockdust. The SEER Centre,
Ceanghline,
Straloch Farm,
Enochdhu,
Perthshire
PH1O 7PJ
Tel. 01250 870 180.
www.seercentre.org.uk

Thought Field Therapy,
Dr. Colin Barron,
50 Kellie Wynd,
Kippendavie,
Dunblane
FK15 ONR
Tel. 01786 821 019
www.thoughtfieldtherapy.co.uk

The Upledger Institute UK   Cranio-sacral therapy
2 Marshall Place,
Perth
PH2 8AH
Tel. 01738 444 404
mail@upledger.co.uk
www.upledger.co.uk